Fr. Marcial Maciel, Pedophile, Psychopath, and Legion of Christ Founder

From
Fr. Richard John Neuhaus
to
Pope Benedict XVI

Fr. Marcial Maciel, Pedophile, Psychopath, and Legion of Christ Founder

From
Fr. Richard John Neuhaus
to Pope Benedict XVI

By
J. Paul Lennon

Fr. Neuhaus Duped by the Legion

of Christ

Revised and augmented

Grateful acknowledgement is made to *First Things*, New York, NY for permission to reproduce passages from articles by the Rev. Richard John Neuhaus.

OPHELIA (to Laertes)

45 I shall the effect of this good lesson keep,
46 As watchman to my heart. But, good my
brother,
47 Do not, as some ungracious pastors do,
48 Show me the steep and thorny way to
heaven,
49 Whiles, like a puff'd and reckless libertine,
50 Himself the primrose path of dalliance
treads,
51 And recks not his own rede.

Hamlet, Act One, Scene 3

By William Shakespeare

PUBLICATIONS
BY J. PAUL LENNON

Our Father Maciel, who art in bed, a Naïve and
Sentimental Dubliner in the Legion of Christ

Book and Kindle form; it also appeared under a
different title:

Our Father, who art in bed, a Naïve and Sentimental
Dubliner in the Legion of Christ

Spanish language spirituality:

Viaje hacia la Pascua, Con el Cristo de los Evangelios

Un Cura Lucha con Dios, Plegarias de Pasión y Locura

PSYCHOPATHY PCL-R items[1]

The following findings are for research purposes only, and are not used in clinical diagnosis. These items cover the affective, interpersonal, and behavioral features. Each item is rated on a score from zero to two. The sum total determines the extent of a person's psychopathy.

Factor 1

Aggressive narcissism

1. Glibness/superficial charm

2. Grandiose sense of self-worth

3. Pathological lying

4. Cunning/manipulative

5. Lack of remorse or guilt

6. Emotionally shallow

7. Callous/lack of empathy

8. Failure to accept responsibility for own actions

---

[1] http://en.wikipedia.org/wiki/Psychopathy

CONTENTS

Preface

A scathing review on Amazon.com hit *R.J. Neuhaus Duped by the Legion of Christ* below the waterline. Hence this second "revised and augmented" vessel. Leaving dry dock the old *Neuhaus Duped* was launched with a new name, the repaired hull sporting streamlined chronology: inserted late reflections were tidied up and consigned to the stern. A discussion of Pope Benedict XVI's comments on the Legion of Christ Founder provided ballast. Maciel's psychology was put under review showing that he was much more than a sexual deviant. An excellent essay by Peter Kingsland on Maciel as an abusive leader pulled the chapters together making for a more seaworthy ship.

The author's brief correspondence with Richard John Neuhaus took place in 2002 as a reaction to his then famous "Feathers of Scandal" defense of Fr. Marcial Maciel, founder of the Legion of Christ, accused of pedophilia. Fr. Neuhaus demonstrated his willingness to engage in correspondence with an unknown minnow of the Catholic world who dared "question him". He was always civil, respectful, and fair in the fray. His pointed questions made me reflect and he, in turn, reflected on my answers.

Those 2002 *corazonadas* - heartfelt intuitions - regarding the immoral life of the Rev. Marcial Maciel - were borne out by subsequent revelations made by the Legion leadership itself, a Vatican Investigation followed by a Reform Intervention, and finally by the words of His Holiness Benedict XVI. Ever since their 1941 foundation Maciel and the Legion had been "a sign of contradiction" in Mexico, the Vatican, Ireland, the USA and many other countries. From the 1960's through the early 21st century the Legion sailed silently and swiftly to forty countries buoyed by the adulation of conservative Catholics. Even after a Vatican investigation into allegation of pedophilia against Fr. Maciel in 2005 and a subsequent slap on the wrist in 2006, many refused to doubt or question, attributing criticism to ill will, hatred, and even a desire to "destroy the Catholic priesthood and the Church". Not long after Maciel's death Legion leadership out of the blue revealed he had lovers and engendered children. Evidence of a cynically double life destroyed Maciel's image in the eyes of the public much more successfully than his detractors had ever hoped. A second Vatican "visitation" of the institution in 2009 put a further dent in the Legion's armor. Pope Benedict XVI in *Light of the World* tried to explain the mystery of Maciel to the faithful while saving the Legion he spawned. Did the pope succeed?

R.J. Neuhaus' Defense of Rev. Maciel, Pedophile Legion of Christ Founder

The Rev. Neuhaus' defense of the Rev. Maciel accused of pedophilia marked an important milestone in the intra-Catholic debate on priestly pedophilia. The Founder of First Things spoke out in favor of the Founder of the Legion of Christ, a powerful media figure coming to the defense of a powerful Church figure, an Orthodox Catholic coming to the aid of an Orthodox Catholic Order, papist pro papist, conservative for conservative. By the time he wrote about Fr. Maciel, Fr. Neuhaus had formed a bond with the Legion of Christ. The genesis of that bond could be the subject of a separate study. Fr. Neuhaus was won over by the Legionaries and he remained faithful to them until the end. He gave their news agency ZENIT exclusive interviews in 2003 and 2005

For many Catholics at that time Neuhaus' opinion was the final word in all things Catholic whether doctrine, morals, culture or politics. His pen carried a lot of clout and his sharp critique of the calumnies against Fr. Maciel did much to stem corroding rumors and innuendos about the holy founder of an order producing edifying priests and apostolic works at a fast and steady pace. Though never overtly stated, the Legion appeared to be the best thing since the Jesuits and Maciel the best thing since Ignatius of Loyola. To besmirch him with the taint of sexual impropriety was unacceptable. R.J. Neuhaus rallied the troops with his ringing sermon against spreading "Feathers of Scandal".

In order to set the stage for my brief correspondence with Fr. Neuhaus I hearken back to *Scandal Time III*[2] where he recapped his previous articles on the clergy sex abuse crisis. I bold content to which I took exception:

"Where We Have Been

Since this is probably not the last installment of 'Scandal Time,' it is worth recalling where we have been and then bring it back to the present. The first installment in April set forth why this really is a crisis, and why it is both false and self-defeating to blame it on the media or anti-Catholicism, or a combination of both. This is our crisis. It cannot be understood apart from the cultural milieu of the sixties when, in a confused concatenation of

---

[2] First Things 125 (Aug-Sept 2002), 85-108

events, the aggiornamento proposed by the Second Vatican Council was hijacked to mean that the Church should conform itself to the culture, just at the time when the culture was being radically deformed. A critical turning point was the organized and public defiance by Catholic theologians and some bishops of Paul VI's encyclical on human sexuality, including contraception, *Humanae Vitae*. The failure of the bishops to respond to that defiance and to vigorously communicate the message of the encyclical constitutes the moment at which the American bishops ceased to be teachers...

The 1968 recognition that the Church's teaching on faith and morals could be defied with impunity ushered in a period of "wink and nudge" also with respect to sexuality, in its sundry expressions. After being hit with scandals, lawsuits, and multimillion-dollar settlements, the bishops, in the early 1990s, tried to bring the situation under control, especially in the seminaries. This met with a measure of success, and it is notable that almost all the known instances of abuse date from the seventies and eighties. When the dam of past episcopal miscreance broke in Boston last January, district attorneys began to be more assertive about the possible complicity of bishops in criminal acts, and bishops felt forced to compromise traditional and legal prerogatives related to the Church's right to

15

govern itself. I observed that the compromising of the right of ecclesial self-governance (*libertas ecclesiae*) may have deeply troubling consequences for the future of the free exercise of religion, and not only for Catholics.

In the second installment (June/July), I noted **that what was at first called a "pedophilia" crisis was now recognized by almost everyone as a crisis created by adult men having sex of various sorts with adolescent and older teenage boys.** The H-word is unavoidable, although many strive mightily to avoid it or to complexify it into oblivion. I surveyed the rapidly accumulating literature in support of the significance of the homosexuality factor, and criticized those who try to change the subject by advocating the relaxation of the discipline of celibacy. I described the role of the Catholic Theological Society of America in promoting deviance from Catholic teaching and the trumping of the doctrinal by the therapeutic. This invited an extended reflection on Philip Rieff's classic work The Triumph of the Therapeutic, and its prescient analysis of what would happen if, after Vatican II, Catholic leaders replaced the spiritual with the psychological (or equated the two), turning therapy into something very much like a new religion. I concluded by saying that Dallas would be a debacle if the bishops did not address in a straightforward manner the three causes of the crisis — infidelity, infidelity, and infidelity."

My personal interest centered on the "Feathers of Scandal" article[3] where Fr. Neuhaus had illustrated the danger of an over-zealous witch-hunt of innocent priests with the example of Fr. Marcial Maciel, founder of the Legion of Christ. According to Fr. Neuhaus Fr. Maciel was being falsely accused by ill-intentioned calumniators. He brilliantly explained this with an anecdote from the life of St. Philip Neri and his sermon on "Feathers of Scandal" —once they are out of the bag, pillow-case, it is impossible to put them all back in again. The reader may remember that eloquent article:

"The story is told of St. Philip Neri (1515–1595) that he gave a most unusual penance to a novice who was guilty of spreading malicious gossip. He told him to take a feather pillow to the top of a church tower on a blustery day and there release all the feathers to the wind. Then he was to come down from the tower, collect all the feathers dispersed over the far countryside, and put them

---

[3] First Things, 121, March, 2002;
http://www.firstthings.com/ftissues/ft0203/public.html
can be read for free at:
http://www.bishop-accountability.org/news/
2002_03_Neuhaus_FeathersOf.htm

back into the pillow. Of course the poor novice couldn't do it, and that was precisely Philip's point about the great evil of tale bearing. Slander and calumny have a way of spreading to the four winds and, once released, can never be completely recalled. Even when accusations are firmly nailed as false, the reputations of those falsely accused bear a lingering taint. 'Oh yes,' it is vaguely said, 'wasn't he once accused of ...'

This reflection is occasioned by an attack on Father Marcial Maciel Degollado, the eighty–two–year–old and much revered founder of the Legionaries of Christ, one of the more vibrant and successful renewal movements in contemporary Catholicism. The attack, alleging sexual offenses with seminarians some forty years earlier, first appeared in a 1997 story in the Hartford Courant, a Connecticut paper, and the story has recently been repeated in the National Catholic Reporter, a left–wing tabloid. The story was coauthored by Jason Berry, a freelance writer in New Orleans, who briefly gained national attention with a 1992 book, *Lead Us Not Into Temptation: Catholic Priests and the Sexual Abuse of Children*, and by Gerald Renner, who was until recently religion writer for the Connecticut paper."

"The Power of Envy

Berry and Renner do not even try to hide their hostility to the Legion. Their story introduces the movement as "a wealthy religious order known for its theological conservatism and loyalty to the Pope." In the world of Berry, Renner, the National Catholic Reporter, and the Courant (at least when Renner was writing for it), that is another way of saying that the Legion is the enemy. Nobody would dispute that Legionaries are theologically orthodox and loyal to the Pope. (…)"

"Recruited to a Cause

I am not neutral about the Legionaries. **I have spent time with Fr. Maciel, and he impresses me as a man who combines uncomplicated faith, gentle kindness, military self–discipline, and a relentless determination to do what he believes God has called him to do.** They are the qualities one would expect of someone who at age twenty–one in Mexico vowed to do something great for Christ and his Church, and has been allowed to do it. In the language of the tradition, they are qualities associated with holiness; in his case a virile holiness of tenacious resolve that has been refined in the fires of frequent opposition and misunderstanding. (…)"

"With Moral Certainty

So what is a person who does not share their

prejudices and purposes to believe? I can only say why, after a scrupulous examination of the claims and counterclaims, **I have arrived at moral certainty that the charges are false and malicious.** I cannot know with cognitive certainty what did or did not happen forty, fifty, or sixty years ago. No means are available to reach legal certainty (beyond a reasonable doubt). Moral certainty, on the other hand, is achieved by considering the evidence in light of the Eighth Commandment, "You shall not bear false witness against your neighbor." On that basis, I believe the charges against Fr. Maciel and the Legion are false and malicious and should be given no credence whatsoever.

Recall the teaching of the Catechism of the Catholic Church in explanation of the Eighth Commandment:

Respect for the reputation of persons forbids every attitude and word likely to cause them unjust injury. He becomes guilty:

— of rash judgment who, even tacitly, assumes as true, without sufficient foundation, the moral fault of a neighbor;

— of detraction who, without objectively valid reason, discloses another's fault and failings to persons who did not know them;

— of calumny who, by remarks contrary to the

truth, harms the reputation of others and gives occasion for false judgments concerning them.

It counts as evidence that Fr. Maciel unqualifiedly and totally denies the charges. It counts as evidence that priests in the Legion whom I know very well and who, over many years, have a detailed knowledge of Fr. Maciel and the Legion say that the charges are diametrically opposed to everything they know for certain. It counts as evidence that Joseph Cardinal Ratzinger and others who have looked into the matter say that the charges are completely without merit. It counts as evidence that Pope John Paul II, who almost certainly is aware of the charges, has strongly, consistently, and publicly praised Fr. Maciel and the Legion. Much of what we know we take on trust. I trust these people. The suggestion that they are either deliberately deceiving or are duped is totally implausible."

Thus spake Richard John Neuhaus in March, 2002.

2

Regarding Pedophilia, Fr. Maciel, and the Legion of Christ

A propos "Scandal Time III", First Things (August-September 2002)[4]

Dear Father Neuhaus,

As a Legion of Christ member for twenty-three years –fifteen as priest- and presently as a mental health therapist, I have a couple of points to make: the first about "Scandal Time III"; the second about Father Maciel, Founder and Superior General of the Legion of Christ. Because of your dim view of psychology and psychologists, and perhaps of ex-priests who have not followed your "fidelity, fidelity, fidelity" precept, I hope you will not dismiss off-hand my person or my opinion.

What is pedophilia?

Let me begin by saying that I agree with you that

---

[4] Fr. Neuhaus' specific defense of Fr. Maciel took place in an article titled "Feathers of Scandal": it was widely used by the Legion and Regnum Christi in English-speaking countries and translated into Spanish and distributed among members and the public in Spain, Mexico, and Latin America.

pedophilia is not a result of celibacy and that marriage does not solve pedophilia, or lust. However, I also believe that pedophilia and homosexuality are two different things. Definitions may help clarify this statement. My point is that your article is lacking in a real knowledge of the nature of pedophilia and goes off onto theological and philosophical tangents that distract from the issue.

Beginning in "The No-Mercy Route" you pick up on journalist Goodstein's image of "seventy-year-old Father X". The Father X hypothesis conjures up this nice old priest who had one "slip" many years ago, repented and never did it again. Now the bishops are going to sacrifice him to their "zero tolerance" policy. You come back to this image several times to show just how unmerciful the bishops' policy is. However, in this instance and in others throughout your article you seem to ignore the true nature of pedophilia, tend to minimize its gravity, and even sometimes appear to "blame the victim".

You also seem to slide from the concepts of pedophilia and ephebophilia to homosexuality, placing them on some kind of a continuum of deviousness. In a previous installment, *Scandal Time Continued* you noted how the pedophilia crisis "was

24

now recognized by almost everyone as a crisis created by adult men having sex of various sorts with adolescent and older teenage boys." I, however, believe there is a consensus among psychologists and moralists that Pedophilia is a peculiar form of sexual abuse involving deception and/or an abuse of power, authority and/or status. The only difference between pedophilia and ephebophilia —which are essentially the sexual abuse of a minor, is the age and developmental stage of the victim: before or after puberty, erection and ejaculation. In other words, whether the offender prefers younger or older minors, and how sexually responsive she/he needs them to be to achieve gratification. I may have overlooked your working definition of pedophilia. A generally accepted definition[6] would be as follows:

"Contacts or interactions between a minor and a person, usually at least five years older, when the minor is being used as an object of gratification for the more powerful individual's sexual needs or desires."

---

[5] Scandal Time Continued, First Things 124 (June/July) 2002, 75-100.
http://www.firstthings.com/article/2009/02/scandal-time-continued-43

[6] Porter, E., *Treating the Young Male Victim of Sexual Assault*, Safer Society Press, 1991

And yes, Father Neuhaus, there is such a thing as "no-contact abuse". This would include voyeurism, exhibitionism, solicitation to sex, and other sexual deviancies. In effect, the "sin" is in the mind and heart of the beholder, as Jesus teaches (Matthew 5, 27-28). Let us remember: pedophilia is not about the actions of the minor but about the reactions and actions of the adult or older, more powerful individual.

The Father X Hypothesis

I consider the benign Father X simile quite devious, especially the way you keep building on what began as a hypothesis. The good Father X takes on a life of his own in your article. Now just let us suppose that Father X had "only one abusive incident with a minor, thirty years ago, that he had repented, that he has put his life back in order..."

That one offense was, nevertheless, very serious. Did he receive appropriate consequences and remedial treatment? Did he apologize to the victim? Did he make reparation as best he could? Did he take a serious look at his behavior and tendencies? Does he, did you and your readers realize that once is too much and that a victim can be scarred for life because of one invasion of boundaries, one -as you would put it- "impure touch" of Christ's little ones.

There is also a kind of "clerical privilege" that pervades the articles. It would seem you are saying: "Let the victim get his therapy and seek healing for being sinfully touched by Fr. X. while Fr. X gets back to the important business of touching the Body and Blood of Christ."

Are we saying that Fr. X. was caught only once? Could there have been other occasions when he was not caught? Were there other accusations and this the only one that stuck? A pedophile is not content with a one-time fix. Real pedophiles are "repeat offenders" and often have multiple victims.

Pedophiles are notoriously "slippery" and usually respond with blanket denial when first confronted. They will stonewall until they are convicted. Many offenses go undetected because the victim is silent or not believed. So offenders usually get a lot of "freebies" before they are caught. How many "freebies" did Father X. get? Non-violent pedophiles usually need to lay elaborate plans and strategies in order to trap a victim. This is called "grooming" and it can take weeks or months. So in this sense there is no real "one time only". It is not a "slip", like the impulsive pinching you described so well. It is more like a pinching you were thinking about for some time. I would call it a "premeditated accidentally-on-purpose slip".

Regarding the Legion and Fr. Maciel

"All that glitters is not gold" as regards the Legion of Christ. Years of experience as a priest and now therapist have led me to be cautious. When someone or something is "Too good to be true", it usually is.

In your article you omitted mention of the sexual abuse allegations against Father Maciel, Founder and Superior General "for life" of the Legion Christ for whom you have a predilection. I was fortunate never to have experienced any sexual abuse while in the Legion. However, I did experience Father Maciel's absolute power in governing, his harshness, his public humiliation, his sarcasm and ridicule when commenting on members' and "outsider's" shortcomings. No one, who knows him closely, except his lackeys, would ever consider him "saint material". I did not want to believe the stories of sex abuse when they first appeared. Not until I had heard the testimonies of his accusers -some of whom I had known personally and had no reason to doubt- did I start to think that something like that could be true. From my point of view, sexual abuse would simply be another form of the abuse of power I had come to associate with Father Maciel. You, in your trips to Rome, etc., have experienced the nice side of the Legion and Father Maciel. You are friendly to their cause. They "wined and dined you", "groomed you" and now they "cultivate you" (until you no longer serve their cause). You are of use to them. You have succumbed to the "Master of Deceit". But you cannot say you know either Father Maciel or the Legion in a thorough way and on a daily basis. You have not lived in community with him for a prolonged period of time. You are impressed by the appearances, by the results, by the glitter...

Regarding the sexual abuse aspect; let me tell you a short story. In 1970, just after our ordination, a colleague of mine was sent as a new superior to the Apostolic School (junior seminary) in Ontaneda, Santander, Spain. Several boys approached him accusing one of the staff, another LC priest, of getting some of the little Spaniards into bed with him. The newly arrived superior knew that Maciel had previously sexually abused the abuser. As a blindly obedient religious, and according to his LC training, he immediately notified Father Maciel. Our Father told the priest in question not to worry; that he would take care of everything. Within hours, the Territorial Director, Fr. Rafael Arumí, was dispatched from Salamanca to Ontaneda. The offending priest was summarily sent packing without any process. At that time the Legion was starting a new apostolate: the Mission Prelature in Chetumal, Quintana Roo, Mexico. The offending priest was sent there. He remains there to this day, if he is still alive. What about the indigenous Maya children under his pastoral care? Do they count?[7]

I, for my part, will not consent with my silence to the continuous endangerment of innocent boys, no matter how apparently holy and worthy the cause.

Paul Lennon STL, MA

---

[7] See Addendum 1, page 109

Richard John Neuhaus replied:

Mr. Paul Lennon

Dear Mr. Lennon, I am familiar with, but not persuaded by, some of the standard distinctions employed in the discussion of sexual deviancies. I appreciate your thoughts on the Legion and Fr. Maciel. Permit me to suggest, however, that you move with startling rapidity from "having no reason to doubt" that "something like that could be true," to the assumption that Fr. Maciel is guilty of the crimes and sins alleged by his accusers. If you have not already, you might search the FIRST THINGS website for the article in which I explain why I do not believe the charges against Fr. Maciel.

Thank you for writing.

Cordially,

(The Rev.) Richard John Neuhaus

3

A Scholastic Response to:

"You are jumping to conclusions regarding Fr. Maciel"

How I Reached My Conclusions Regarding Fr. Maciel Sexually Abusing his Seminarians

"Father Neuhaus:

Thanks for replying so quickly to my letter to the editor. I appreciate your interest in the issues at hand and your willingness to engage in an enlightened discussion. Let me just make a couple of replies to your replies, which I will insert for the sake of clarity.

2.1 I *am familiar with, but not persuaded by, some of the standard distinctions employed in the discussion of sexual deviancies.*

Respondeo dicendum quod;

Primum: I believe you were the one who in your article referred to distinctions such as "pedophilia" and "ephebophilia". I pointed out before that when there is a serious discrepancy in age/power/ authority/knowledge between those engaging in sexual activities such behavior is generally considered "AN ABUSIVE RELATIONSHIP", and results, for treatment purposes, in one of the parties being considered "the perpetrator" and the other "the victim".

Secundum: I did not use the term "sexual deviancies", as it is nebulous, and belongs to a more academic, philosophical and psychological realm which would lead to endless intellectual discussions.. I believe I referred to "sexual abuse" in my letter to you. This is more concrete, morally and legally.

2.2 I appreciate your thoughts on the Legion and Fr. Maciel. Permit me to suggest, however, that you move with startling rapidity from "having no reason to doubt" that "something like that could be true," to the assumption that Fr. Maciel is guilty of the crimes and sins alleged by his accusers.

As regards Father Maciel's sexually abusive behaviors, respondeo dicendum quod;

Primum: When I was a Legionary I only heard about the investigations (1956-9) of Father Maciel in and through superiors who were loyal to him: Frs. Rafael Arumí, Octavio Acevedo, Alfredo Torres, Juan Manuel Dueñas, et al. The nature and causes of "La Guerra" (The War) - in Legion parlance of the early 1960s - was never explained to members, except to attribute them to "enemies" "trying to destroy the Legion." The term applied to that Vatican investigation has been revised since then to "La Gran Bendición" (The Great Blessing). Nothing of a sexual nature regarding the troubles of those years was ever mentioned within my hearing. We were told that a number of early Legionaries rebelled against Father Maciel because they were ill-intentioned and wanted to "destroy the Legion". The gist of the story was that they had gotten too big for their boots and began to oppose Fr. Maciel, the Founder. While inside the Legion - 23 years - I never heard anything about the true nature of the accusations against Father Maciel.

There was an informal list of "traitors" which circulated hush-hush through the superiors and was gossiped in the community: names like the Isla brothers, Federico Dominguez, Legaza, a certain Rizo, and others I vaguely remember. Jose Barba, one of the accusers, was from that same generation, but I know he was not considered a "traitor" to Nuestro Padre. Later, in the 1980s, I learned Jose had left the Legion on friendly terms and made a pretty good transition into the academic world. As a matter of fact, Fr. Amenábar once brought me and another Legionary of the time to visit former LC Jose Barba when he has teaching at a university (Universidad de las Américas)) in Puebla, Mexico.

Secundum: I, personally, had no inkling of any sexual abuse in the Legion. But while a member, 1961-1984 I had personally known at least five of Father Maciel's accusers: Arturo Jurado, Felix Alarcón, Juan Jose Vaca, Jose Barba and Juan Manuel Amenábar, in varying degrees of closeness. I never had a personal conversation with any of them because I was younger and did not "belong to their community" and was prohibited by the Norms from having any communication with them. And besides, Legionaries are so guarded in their interpersonal disclosure, that even if I had been their direct confrere, I would probably not have learned anything either. Legion Norms would also preclude the accusers discussing their abuse among themselves while in the Legion. The Private Vow –never to criticize a superior in any way and to inform on whoever did this- was drafted just before the 1956-59 Vatican investigation began and ratified soon after. I am not sure whether Fr. Maciel did this purposely to nip any criticism or revelations quickly in the proverbial bud.

"Knowing" the accusers explains how, when I read the first articles in 1998, the victims were not just names to me, and I had to take them seriously. But I still doubted, or did not want to believe, that I had been so close to something as outrageous as pedophilia. On the other hand I "knew" Father Maciel much better than later members. He had been a part of my life since he traveled with the first Irish group to Lourdes in August 1961. He had heard my "general confession" before my taking the habit, and had heard my regular confession on several occasions; I had exchanged Spiritual Direction Letters with him on a monthly basis for about 20 years, and had face to face Spiritual Direction on several occasions. I had more frequent dealings with Father Maciel when he chose me to found and direct the "School of Faith" in Mexico City, 1975-82. I had some tussles of authority with him from the 1980s on. Finally, I had confronted him in Cotija, Michoacán, in the fall of 1984 regarding the fate of those who disagree or leave the institution. We lashed out at each other.[8]

Tertium: Last year when I listened to Barba and Vaca tell me their stories over the phone -

---

[8] Two year later I would write in my journal *An Enigma to Me*; see Addendum 2, page 111; I describe this episode in *Our Father Maciel who art in bed*, Amazon, 2008

separately and without the other knowing - I was very moved by their undeniable pain, shame and honesty. I met them both earlier this (2002) year, together with Jurado, in conjunction with the 20/20 TV interviews in New York and became more convinced of the truth of their persons and testimony. I saw with my own eyes how they were re-traumatized by the harrowing lengthy TV interviews - which produced just a few moments of air time! I have read Alarcon's letter describing his abuse and apologizing to the others for his collaboration with Maciel and it rang true. All the pieces fell into place without that having been rehearsed. The details of the places they referred to, of the others involved... all sounded real and true.

Quartum: I find it very hard to believe that these men would willingly deceive me. I find it even more difficult to understand why any man at their age, and without benefit to himself, should want to reveal such an intimate and painful part of his life, if it were not true. I find it even harder to believe that they would make up stories that in some cases "incriminate" themselves as accomplices of these crimes (one admits having called other brothers into the infirmary to be fondled, masturbated and sodomized by Father Maciel) unless they were still struggling with the aftermath of untreated abuse and still needed to ventilate their trauma.

Your "incredulous" response is common and does not surprise me. The spontaneous, "natural", response to talk of sexual abuse is denial and minimization. Where a priest is concerned it makes it just that more "incredible" and "impossible". But we have to admit that some priests commit these horrendous crimes. I believe Father Bruce Ritter, the Founder of Covenant House, overstepped boundaries with some youth during his apostolate[9] - though this does not prevent me continuing to support this worthy charity. I believe Father Maciel, despite his marvelous social skills and wonderful gifts as entrepreneur, also committed sexual abuse. But he gets off Scot free thanks to having powerful friends which he has cultivated so well and carefully over the years. Thanks also to the knee-jerk reaction of "it can't be true!" and other forms of unexamined denial from the public in general, and from the conservative right wing Catholic public in particular.

Quintum: Not to make a big deal out of this, but in hindsight some things begin making sense to me. I was a witness to very clear favoritism of Father Maciel towards certain "brothers", who happened to be good-looking or possessed better social skills

---

[9] Charles M. Sennott, 1992, *Broken Covenant*, New York: Simon & Schuster

and graces in the communities where I belonged[10]. In the 1960's and 70's we had much more exposure to Fr. Maciel's presence in the community (of consecrated religious living in the house). This was true specifically in Rome. Nuestro Padre had his own room on the 2nd floor and would be up and about the house, in the corridors and in the gardens conducting business. We could bump into him any time during the day.

CONCLUSION:

All that has been said up to now cannot strictly "prove" Fr. Maciel is a sexual abuser or pedophile. But the least it should do is give you pause, Fr. Neuhaus, before foolhardily endorsing him without sufficient information. The accusers stand steadfast by their claims, despite the tepid response of the Roman Curia and many Catholic writers. Most, if not all, active Legionaries and Regnum Christi members aggressively defend a Father Maciel they have never personally met. Several ex-Legionaries with up close and personal experiences give credence to the charges. I firmly believe truth-searchers, like you, should continue to question Fr. Maciel and themselves regarding these "questionable" relationships with his seminarians. Because of the serious doubts that remain

---

[10] See *Maciel's Favorites*, Addendum 3, page 113

regarding these relationships, it is not unreasonable to seek another "injunction" against him until these doubts have been cleared up. When such charges were made against the Cardinal Archbishop of Perth, Australia, he stepped down until they finished.

I have been able to read the testimonies in the original Spanish as well as in English and this can also have a bearing on their efficacy. I have also personally met the witnesses and spoken with them in their native language. Perhaps there is also an element of "faith" in believing the "testimonies" of the accusers. But that is precisely what "faith" is all about: "believing witnesses", "eye-witnesses", "participants", if possible. I do believe the testimonies of these confreres in their accusations against Marcial Maciel.

Richard John Neuhaus replied:

Thursday, 12 September 2002 16:57:33 -0500
Subject: LC

From: "Richard John Neuhaus"
To: irishmexican43@yahoo.com
Mr. Paul Lennon
Dear Mr. Lennon,
I thank you for your thoughtful response.
*Not for the sake of argument, but because I would really
like to understand: Why do you think the accusers have
come forward at this time and in this way? If they had the
access they seek in Rome, what would they say they think
should be done with regard to Fr. Maciel and the LC, and
why?*
Sincerely,
(The Rev.) Richard John Neuhaus

4

Fr. Neuhaus: *Why (did the accusers) wait until now and with what intentions?*

Dear Father Neuhaus, thanks for the continuing dialogue. Am I right in believing that your defense of Father Maciel in First Things was a response the Renner-Berry article in the NCR in December 2001? And was it based on your limited knowledge of Father Maciel and the inner workings of the Legion?

I will attempt to answer the questions you raised in responding to my previous letter. I take the liberty of doing so because you have not published my previous critique of your article in your magazine. I believe the answers I try to formulate are already somehow present in the "accusers" writings with which you are already somewhat familiar.

I would also like to mention there is at least one important document that has not been translated into English and therefore not available to the English speaking public. It is an "Open Letter to the Pope" written in November 1997 when the "accusers" made a conjoint formal effort to reach the Pope and Vatican authorities with their "case against" Fr. Maciel.

In the following essay I stand corrected by the "witnesses" more precise knowledge of facts and circumstances.

4.1 Why did the accusers wait until now?

Which "now" are you referring to? The Hartford Courant articles of 1997 or the consistent previous attempts to reach the Vatican? The short answer is: they have been writing and speaking for decades but nobody was listening or paying any attention. It was only after the articles appeared in the Courant that they started getting some publicity, credibility and attention. They despair of ecclesiastical action and want to pressure church authorities to do something to hold Father Maciel accountable for his past actions before Father Maciel dies, and/or before they die.

Accusations against or rumors about Father Maciel and his sexual behavior towards junior seminarians were known inside the religious community since he was in Mexico City with the first group of students (c.1940) when the father of one of his boys confronted him (the boy was sent home but his brothers remained). Another cluster of accusations/rumors stem from the time he was in Comillas, Northern Spain with his boys (c.1947). The recent accusations that have reached the Press and TV refer to behavior in the Collegio Massimo, Major Seminary, in Rome in the early 50's and are different in the sense that witnesses have come forward and given sworn testimony. These abuses are described by Alejandro Espinosa in lurid detail in his recent book, "El Legionario" (not yet translated into English).

Just like with any "movement", the "accusers" efforts have taken a long time to gel. We know that they probably did not discuss these issues among themselves while in the Legion. There was the private vow and even a more radical tradition about not discussing personal issues with confreres. Besides, Marcial Maciel had sworn each individual victim to secrecy and he was the supreme authority. Barba, vg, states that MM told him not to mention what happened between them to Father Lagoa, the rector in Rome at that time because "he would not understand". Some of these students were in different stages of "formation", that is "Novitiate", "Juniorate" (Humanities), Philosophy student, etc., and so did not speak to each other across community lines. Though several may have belonged to the same "community"; Vaca reports that he was told to go and summon other brothers to the infirmary, and he would hardly do that across section lines.

The investigation of Father Maciel and the Legion in 1955/56 which led to the Vatican investigation did in fact stem from his visible and unusual attraction for some of the junior seminarians and from other issues such as use of morphine, fund-raising and money. The Vatican "visitors", sent by the Sacred Congregation for Religious, naturally questioned the students about Father Maciel's behavior. The students were too ashamed, immature, ignorant, and afraid or felt a sense of loyalty to Father Maciel to mention any sexual misbehavior. Remember that at the time of the investigations Father Maciel had been the father, sole provider, confidant, spiritual director and principal educator of the students since they were 11 years old or younger. When questioned they would not say anything to incriminate Father Maciel or to jeopardize the Legion and their vocations in it. They had been told that the visitors were coming to "destroy the Legion".

Later, and at different times in the late 1950's and early 60s', some "accusers" left or were dismissed from the Legion individually. The leaving was usually orchestrated to be sudden and quiet, late at night, early morning, when the community was at prayer, in Mass, or otherwise busy. One was not allowed to tell companions that he was leaving. And so each one went home to his town or village and was never heard of again and they did not speak to each other again. (That is the way it was, the way I witnessed it, and the way it still is). Others stayed in the Legion for some time after their abuse: Juan José Vaca, Félix Alarcón, Miguel Díaz, and Juan-Manuel Fernández-Amenábar.... Naturally, there would be absolutely no contact between the ones who left and those who stayed, and probably no intra-group confidences among each other in the group that stayed. That would be against the "private vows" in a very serious way as it meant criticizing the Founder. Besides, to what superior would they reveal it, when the vow obliged them to voice their concerns to the top LC superior, and this would have been the perpetrator himself?

Juan Jose Vaca, an assertive type, is the one who probably demonstrated most awareness and courage in directly and formally demanding accountability while still a member of the Legion and a subject of Maciel. Despite having a prolonged sexual relationship with his superior and being Maciel's "accomplice" in procuring more victims for him, he questioned Maciel on several occasions about the morality of their actions. This would be almost apologetically along the lines of: "Father, I don't feel good about these actions. I know you absolved me and told me not to worry, but..." As he got older and more uncomfortable he began confronting Fr. Maciel as early as the 1960's when the Mexican bishops were staying at the Collegio Massimo on Via Aurelia Nova 677 during the Vatican Council II. He says Maciel minimized the issues but gave him an interesting position (in charge of logistics for the 30 Mexican bishops, with freedom to move in and out of the community, do the shopping, and go on errands to the Vatican...). Vaca confronted Maciel again around the time of his priestly ordination (1969). Soon after ordination Maciel made Vaca –who spoke English because he had spent some time in Ireland– superior of the Legion in the US. When Vaca was on his way out of the Legion in the 70's and threatened to expose Maciel the latter supposedly tried to bribe Vaca offering him any position he wanted in the Legion.

After Vaca left the Legion and was in the diocese of Rockville Center he approached his pastor, and later his bishop who sent documentation to Rome by courier (via de Vatican Embassy in Washington, 1978). In the 1980's Vaca received his dispensation from celibacy and was married in the NY area; he lives there with his wife and daughter. He did not return to his native Mexico for many years and so did not have much contact with Legionaries or ex-Legionaries to "plot with them."

José de Jesús Barba, for his part, made a "good" transition out of the Legion before ordination much earlier, around 1962. He had always been a "brain" and "idealistic"; after leaving he was able to study at Harvard and got his doctorate. Returning to Mexico he kept contact with the Legion, even working for a while as a teacher at the Anahuac University. He was friendly with people inside and outside the Legion and had an encyclopedic memory for events. In the 1970's, when he was married with children, he must have started to remember and face up to his own sexual abuse. At first he thought he was the only one. When he started opening up others told him that they too had been victims. Nobody was very keen on coming forward. They wanted to keep their secret buried and get on with their lives. He would not let it rest and found some echo in Alejandro Espinoza, José Antonio Pérez-Olvera and others in Mexico and in Jurado who was working in San Diego. Vaca and Barba approached several others they knew had been victims but these did not want to testify; they preferred to remain anonymous and so were never mentioned in any public statements. Around the 1990s the group started to gather momentum when Barba and Vaca began making contact and discussing their efforts. Barba, for his part, in Mexico had started to write and approach ecclesiastical authorities. Barba had maintained his ties with ex-confrere Amenábar who was ill at the Sanatorio Español hospital in Mexico City. There was a Mexican diocesan priest who heard Amenábar's confession and confidences, Father Athié, who held a position in the Archbishop of Mexico's curia. He became convinced that Amenábar wanted to tell his story before he died. Felix Alarcón, who was aware of Vaca's accusations and had confirmed them to Rockville Center authorities, still an active priest, when contacted was willing to admit his abuse[11].

The witnesses agreed to speak to the press when approached by the Hartford Courant reporter who had previously picked up on some unusual happenings at the Legion's novitiate in CT, i.e. novices "escaping" over the wall. The victims spoke with the reporters because they were frustrated with not getting a satisfactory response from local ecclesiastical authorities in Mexico, being told to wait, to "leave it in God's hands", to "forgive and forget" "wait until Father Maciel dies" or sworn to secrecy... and by Rome's silence.

When Father Maciel was called "a leader and defender of youth" by the Pope they became more indignant and galvanized to write an open letter to the Pope lodging a formal complaint at the Vatican.

---

[11] See Addendum 4, page 115

4.2   *What did they expect from the Vatican?*

They wanted an independent investigation into the allegations. They accused Father Maciel of breaking several canons, of sexually abusing them and of absolving them after the abuse (absolutio complicis, Canon Law, number 1378). Corresponding sanctions would cause him to be defrocked and excommunicated.

They wanted the Vatican to review the Constitutions and Traditions of the Legion, and to investigate and reform Legion practices. To have a "clean" General Chapter without the ever- present pressure and control of Maciel.

Many ex-Legionaries and ex-Regnum Christi wish: that Church Authorities examine and investigate the behavior of Father Maciel and the Legionaries of Christ, particularly the way it recruits, retains and controls members and later handles dissident and exiting members.

Because Father Maciel, the official church, and the Vatican are stonewalling and avoiding accountability, the victims are (were) getting more and more frustrated and some of them have begun to write their individual memoirs as a last resort to redress their abuse before they die.

SUMMARIZING:

The testimonies of the eight living ex-members accusing Father Maciel of sexual assault must be read in the context of the founder's charismatic powers of persuasion and manipulation, and the Legion's private vows of family secrecy, solidarity, and control: this control, during and after membership, limited the possibility of a conspiracy to a large extent. The youth, powerlessness and inexperience of the victims at the time of the abuse should also be taken into consideration.

Sincerely,
J. Paul Lennon MA

Fr. Neuhaus' Response

(Circa 17/18 September, 2002)

Mr. J. Paul Lennon

Dear Mr. Lennon,

Thank you for your further responses to my questions.

You have given me much to think about, and I will be doing that.

Cordially,

(The Rev.) Richard John Neuhaus

THANKS

Date: Wed, 18 Sep 2002 16:49:19 -700 (PDT)

From: J. Paul Lennon

Subject: Re: thanks

To: Richard John Neuhaus

Father Neuhaus:

I appreciate your interest, time, and the honest dialogue. May the Holy Spirit guide us in these delicate matters. Do not think that I never question my own intentions and honesty in these very serious issues, especially when I realize that I am a small minority among many who have great respect for Father Maciel. I think you referred to him as "venerable" or "revered" or something. But I like many others who had him on a pedestal, lost respect for him down through the years based on his behavior. Do not forget that I, too, was "trained" as a Legionary for many years and taught never to speak ill of others. Unfortunately, I can tell you that when Father Maciel "lets his hair down" with an intimate group around the table, with a glass of Johnny Walker "red label" -in his hand, he does not always practice what he so lavishly preaches. Then there is much talk of "friends" and "enemies" of the Legion, and the "enemies" are fair game, no matter who they are. Regarding the sexual abuse, when I hear my brothers" testimonies I continue to feel sad and indignant. Maybe –from your point of view- I give them too much credence, but that is where I am, what I am, and who I am.

Sincerely,

J. Paul Lennon, MA
Alexandria, VA

5

Revisiting the 2006 Vatican Censure of Fr. Maciel and Fr. Neuhaus' Interpretation

In May, 2006 the Vatican released a statement regarding Fr. Maciel, Founder, and for 60 years Superior General, of the Legion of Christ. Was the Vatican solving the controversy and resolving our debate? Fr. Neuhaus liked to have the last word and so we reproduce his interpretation of the Vatican statement - his mature opinion four years after our discussion.

Vatican City (May 19, 2006) (VIS)

With reference to recent news concerning the person of Fr. Marcial Maciel Degollado, founder of the Legionaries of Christ, the Holy See Press Office released the following communiqué:

"Beginning in 1998, the Congregation for the Doctrine of the Faith received accusations, already partly made public against Fr. Marcial Maciel Degollado, founder of the Congregation of the Legionaries of Christ, for crimes that fall under the exclusive competence of the congregation. In 2002, Fr. Maciel published a declaration denying the accusations and expressing his displeasure at the offence done him by certain former Legionaries of Christ. In 2005, by reason of his advanced age, Fr. Maciel retired from the office of superior general of the Congregation of the Legionaries of Christ. "All these elements have been subject to a mature examination by the Congregation for the Doctrine of the Faith and - in accordance with the *Motu Proprio Sacramentorum sanctitatis tutela,* promulgated on April 30 2001 by Servant of God John Paul II - the then prefect of the Congregation for the Doctrine of the Faith, Cardinal Joseph Ratzinger, authorized an investigation into the accusations. In the meantime, Pope John II died and Cardinal Ratzinger was elected as the new Pontiff.

"After having attentively studied the results of the investigation, the Congregation for the Doctrine of the Faith, under the guidance of the new prefect, Cardinal William Joseph Levada, decided - bearing in mind Fr. Maciel's advanced age and his delicate health - to forgo a canonical hearing and to invite the father to a reserved life of penitence and prayer, relinquishing any form of public ministry. The Holy Father approved these decisions.

"Independently of the person of the Founder, the worthy apostolate of the Legionaries of Christ and of the Association 'Regnum Christi' is gratefully recognized."

Fr. Richard John Neuhaus Interprets

May 19, 2006[12]

The Congregation for the Doctrine of the Faith (CDF), with the approval of the Holy Father, has decided, in the words of the official Vatican statement, "to invite (Father Marcial Maciel) to a reserved life of penitence and prayer, relinquishing any form of public ministry."

Fr. Maciel is the founder of the Legionaries of Christ and its lay association, Regnum Christi. He retired from active leadership in 2005. Beginning in 1998, a number of charges of sexual wrongdoing, related to events of five decades ago, were brought against Fr. Maciel by former members of the Legion. The CDF conducted an investigation of the charges but, because of Fr. Maciel's fragile health and advanced age, did not conduct a canonical hearing. Since there was no

---

[12] http://www.firstthings.com/onthesquare/?p=263

canonical hearing, there is no canonical judgment regarding his guilt or innocence of the alleged wrongdoings.

The most precise statement of what has happened, I believe, is that, in the judgment of CDF and the pope, it is in the best interests of the Church, the Legion, and Fr. Maciel that he relinquish his public ministry and devote the remainder of his life to penitence and prayer. It should be noted that "penitence" in this connection does not connote punishment for wrongdoing. The Vatican statement also says that "the worthy apostolate of the Legionaries of Christ and of the association Regnum Christi is gratefully recognized."

What to make of all this? Although, I have no formal connection with the Legion and Regnum Christi, I have over the years been a strong supporter of both. They have in the past, do now, and, I am confident, will continue to provide vibrant apostolate in the service of Christ and his Church. When the charges against Fr. Maciel first surfaced, I studied the matter with care and had detailed discussions with knowledgeable people on all sides of the ensuing controversy. I said in First Things and elsewhere that I was "morally certain" the charges were false. Moral certitude, it should be noted, is a very high degree of probability that justifies action, but is short of certitude described as absolute, mathematical, or metaphysical. I do not know all that the CDF and the Holy Father know, and am not privy to the considerations that led to their decision. It is reasonable to believe that they think Fr. Maciel did do something wrong.

The official statement of the Legion says: "Fr. Maciel, with the spirit of obedience to the Church that has always characterized him, has accepted this communiqué with faith, complete serenity, and tranquility of conscience, knowing that it is a new cross that God, the Father of Mercy, has allowed him to suffer and that will obtain many graces for the Legion of Christ and the Regnum Christi Movement. The Legionaries of Christ and the members of Regnum Christi, following the example of Fr. Maciel and united to him, accept and will accept always the directives of the Holy See with a profound spirit of obedience and faith. We renew our commitment to work with great intensity to live our charisma of charity and extend the Kingdom of Christ serving the Church."

The Legion statement also says, "Facing the accusations made against him, (Fr. Maciel) declared his innocence and, following the example of Christ, decided not to defend himself in any way." The venerable spiritual tradition being followed here is that of purification through suffering, in the confidence that Fr. Maciel will one day be vindicated. There is ample historical precedent of holy men and women who were unjustly treated by church authorities, St. Joan of Arc, for an obvious instance. Or the eleventh-century saint, Pope Gregory VII, whose dying words were, "I loved righteousness, I hated iniquity, and so I die in exile."

It was hardly the only factor, but one of the many factors that entered into my moral certainty regarding Fr. Maciel's innocence was my great respect for John Paul II and his repeated statements of support for Fr. Maciel. With similar respect for the office and person of Pope Benedict, I do not protest this directive implying that Fr. Maciel is guilty of wrongdoing. It is obvious that CDF and the Holy Father know more than I know with respect to evidence supporting the guilt or innocence of Fr. Maciel.

I earnestly pray that the magnificent apostolate of the Legion of Christ and of Regnum Christi will continue to flourish in the service of Christ and his Church.

6

End of Debate?

I was naive when I thought the Vatican communiqué of May, 2006, ordering Fr. Maciel to a life of penance and prayer would make our discussion mute. We see above how Fr. Neuhaus interpreted it and 2006 until 2009 it was interpreted benignly by the Legion (Superior General Corcuera, Secretary General Sada) and its supporters (Veronica Wilkins from COMPASS, Massimo Introvigne from CESNUR, R.J. Neuhaus, et al.)[13]. Victims and critics remained frustrated. However, many who refused to accept that Fr. Maciel was a predatory pedophile have changed their position after revelations in early 2009 that he had lovers and fathered children.

Personally, I do not see how the Legion Founder's sexual relations with women prove that he was a pedophile or a sexual pervert. But maybe logic and reason have not been the order of the day during this debate. Positions were taken a priori for the most part. Even Fr. Neuhaus' reasons for defending Fr. Maciel were vague and a priori. But

---

[13] *Fr. Maciel's Defenders of the Faith*
http://www.regainnetwork.org/article.php?a=47245974

as they came from a person of authority among the Catholic intelligentsia they were taken as Gospel truth by Maciel's defenders. Such defensive stances had a lot to do with what Maciel and the Legion represented to a number of "Orthodox" and fervent Catholics. The Legion was perceived as a bastion of Catholic Orthodoxy, full of handsome, clean-shaven, clerically dressed seminarians and priests, growing in stature and grace before Pope and man. People defended Fr. Maciel's innocence passionately, one might almost say vehemently, and attacked his accusers, those obscure little old Mexican men who were aided and abetted by "liberal reporters" and media, and by rabble-rousing ex-members who dared sully the saint's reputation. John Paul Lennon[14] and REGAIN, INC, who had not ceased to criticize and question the Founder and the Foundation, were sued by the Legion as late as August, 2007. A comment by a Legion supporter on Lennon's YouTube video[15] read: "You got what you deserved!"

---

[14] The author went on to publish *Our Father Maciel, who art in bed. A Naïve and Sentimental Dubliner in the Legion of Christ.*
[15]   http://www.youtube.com/watch?v=hWmajxclRW8
Since revelations of Fr. Maciel's double, triple or multiple lives and official Legion acceptance of such, attacks from pro-Legion troops have subsided for the most part. Derogatory postings were quietly removed by mostly anonymous aggressors.

Today in a calmer vein one can wonder how and why did the presumably wise and knowledgeable Fr. Neuhaus stand by Fr. Marcial Maciel against accusations of pedophilia. How was Fr. Neuhaus taken in by Fr. Maciel, by the Legion of Christ and the Regnum Christi? The body of this booklet features the author's "mano a mano" with RJN, that blinding beacon of catholic learning many feared to question. How do the passage of time and the latest revelations about the double life of Fr. Maciel color, alter or illuminate that previous discussion?

But Fr. Neuhaus still has his defenders and who better than Kevin Staley-Joyce on *First Thoughts* as recently as April 1st, 2010 –perhaps not a propitious day to defend someone who had been April-fooled by Fr. Maciel and the Legion. But defend RJN he does[16]. And who am I to object to a defender of the deceased? Staley-Joyce engages Tim Rutten of the *Los Angeles Times* in battle. He ends with a wise and prophetic quote from Fr. Neuhaus in 2006:

"The future of the Legion and Regnum Christi cannot depend on the innocence or guilt of Fr.

---

[16] *Connecting the Dots on Maciel*
http://www.firstthings.com/blogs/firstthoughts/2010/04/01/connecting-the-dots-on-maciel/

Maciel. Founder and charism may not be entirely separable, but they can be clearly distinguished.

The months and years ahead must be a time of profound self-examination, reform, and renewal. Earnestly and confidently I pray, and invite all to pray, that the magnificent apostolates of the Legion of Christ and Regnum Christi will continue to flourish in the service of Christ and his Church."[17]

The above appear to be Fr. Neuhaus' chronologically last words on Fr. Maciel and the Legion of Christ. He was torn, he wavered; one might even say he hedged his bets. RJN did not want to give up on Fr. Maciel and the Legion of Christ, the Regnum Christi and its apostolates. What is significant about the last words of this Catholic Encyclopedia of a man is that Legion leadership took them to heart. I submit that Neuhaus was the perfect intellectual champion for the Legion, a match on earth made by Marcial Maciel. When in 2009, years after *Their Father's* death, the scandal about his double life had to be revealed; Legion leadership followed their defender's advice:

17 Personal Charism and the Legionaries of Christ in:
Checks, Balances, and Bishops
http://www.firstthings.com/article/2009/03/checks-balances-and-bishops-31

"The future of the Legion and Regnum Christi cannot depend on the innocence or guilt of Fr. Maciel. Founder and charism may not be entirely separable, but they can be clearly distinguished."

Like good disciples, Legion Leadership, Frs. Corcuera, Garza, and Sada went a step beyond their guide; they proposed to separate the Founder and the charism. But in this suggestion I stand to be corrected by sharper and more perceptive minds. Minds like Richard John Neuhaus, R.I.P.

Vatican Chief Investigator Interprets Fr. Maciel's censure in March, 2010

"Cardinal William Joseph Levada decided – bearing in mind Fr. Maciel's advanced age and his delicate health - to forgo a canonical hearing and to invite the father to a reserved life of penitence and prayer, relinquishing any form of public ministry. The Holy Father approved these decisions."

Who is right? What is the proper interpretation of the May 19th, 2006 Vatican statement that came after more than a year's investigation into allegations of sexual improprieties by Fr. Maciel? Gallons of ink have flowed and reams of paper have been used on this debate. Should it be interpreted lightly or heavily, benignly or severely? Some of us believe that the very person who led the investigation and was involved in the "sentence" has recently shed some light in the darkness.

Among my souvenirs is the business card Monsignor Scicluna gave me on April 2nd, 2005 when he met with Juan Jose Vaca and me at the Church of Our Savior, Park Avenue, NY. He took our depositions regarding the life, customs, character and actions of Fr. Marcial Maciel. The plain "6 ½ x "4 ½"card simply says:

Mons. Charles J. Scicluna
Promotore di Giustizia
Congregazione per la Dottrina della Fede
00120 Città del Vaticano

This small, bespeckled and unassuming man, with a streak of assertiveness, and possessing a clear, detailed, and perceptive mind, listened attentively to our testimonies.

Six years later, on Tuesday, March 12, 2011 the same quiet man who avoids the spotlight gave an interview to clear up misconceptions about how Pope Benedict XVI has handled priestly pedophilia. The "affable and polite Maltese" has the reputation of scrupulously carrying out the tasks entrusted to him "without deferring to anyone" - according to the Italian newspaper *L' Avvenire*[18] - as he prepares to take on the new cases rocking the Vatican. The context of the interview was that Benedict had been too lenient with clergy sex offenders. Scicluna explained how the Vatican's prosecuting arm operates and the meanings of the censures it hands down.

He does not refer to the Maciel case explicitly but the following quote is as close as he will ever come publicly:

"Overall in the last nine years we have considered accusations concerning around 3,000 cases of diocesan and religious priests, which refer to crimes committed over the last 50 years...

From these 3,000 cases, some 20% have seen a full trial, penal or administrative, taking place in the diocese of origin under the supervision of the Congregation.

In 60% of cases there has been no trial, "above all because of the advanced age of the accused, but administrative and disciplinary provisions have been issued against them, such as the obligation not to celebrate Mass with the faithful, not to hear confession, and to live a retired life of prayer."

And here, in my opinion, is the clincher in the

---

[18] Official organ of the Italian Bishops Conference, http://www.avvenire.it/Chiesa/intervista+pedofilia+sciclu na_201003130801409170000.htm; the interview appeared simultaneously in the Vatican Information Service: http://www.vatican.va/resources/resources_mons-scicluna-2010_en.html

Maciel case:

"It must be made absolutely clear that in these cases, some of which are particularly sensational and have caught the attention of the media, no absolution has taken place. It's true that there has been no formal condemnation, but if a person is obliged to a life of silence and prayer, then there must be a reason." Two weeks after Monsignor Scicluna's interview by veteran Italian journalist Gianni Cardinale, and three weeks after the Vatican Visitators' Communique Legion leaders would release an admission of their founder's guilt.

7

Legionaries of Christ Apologize

Founder's Actions Called "Reprehensible"

The Vatican ordered an apostolic visitation of the institutions of the Legionaries of Christ following 2009 disclosures of sexual impropriety by the order's late founder, Fr. Marcial Maciel Degollado.

The announcement of the unusual investigation was posted on the Web site of the Legionaries of Christ March 31, along with the text of a letter informing the Legionaries of the pope's decision.

Two months before the results of the Vatican investigation were made public the Legion posted its own statement. Apparently, the leadership must have known the content of the impending communication. Did the Vatican tell the Legion to say something or did the leadership want to forewarn the members of the unsavory results? Only insiders to these maneuvers would know whether this was a pre-emptive strike to take the sting out of the investigations' findings. Let us hear the Legion's communiqué and follow it with the official Vatican version of the results.

COMMUNIQUÉ
regarding the current circumstances of the Legion of Christ and the Regnum Christi Movement

March 25, 2010
Solemnity of the Annunciation of the Lord

Introduction

As we are gathered for the annual meeting of the territorial directors with our general director, we wish to write to our brothers in the Legion of Christ, to the consecrated and all the members of Regnum Christi, our families and friends who accompany us at this juncture in our history, and also to all those who have been affected, wounded, or scandalized by the reprehensible actions of our founder, Fr. Marcial Maciel, LC.

It has taken us time to come to terms with these facts regarding his life. For many, especially the victims, this time has been too long and very painful.

We have not always been able, or found the way to reach out to everyone in the way we should have, and in fact wanted to. Hence the need we feel to make this communiqué.

1. Regarding some facts in the life of our founder, Fr. Marcial Maciel, LC (1920-2008)

We had thought and hoped that the accusations brought against our founder were false and unfounded, since they conflicted with our experience of him personally and his work. However, on May 19, 2006, the Holy See's Press Office issued a communiqué as the conclusion of a canonical investigation that the Congregation for the Doctrine of the Faith (CDF) had begun in 2004. At that time, the CDF reached sufficient moral certainty to impose serious canonical sanctions related to the accusations made against Fr. Maciel, which included the sexual abuse of minor seminarians. Therefore, though it causes us consternation, we have to say that these acts did take place.

Indeed, "the Congregation for the Doctrine of the Faith, (...), mindful of Father Maciel's advanced age and his delicate health, decided to forgo a canonical hearing and ask him to retire to a private life of penance and prayer, giving up any form of public ministry. The Holy Father approved these decisions" (Communiqué of the Press Office of the Holy See, May 19, 2006).

We later came to know that Fr. Maciel had fathered a daughter in the context of a prolonged and stable relationship with a woman, and committed other grave acts. After that, two other people surfaced, blood brothers who say they are his children from his relationship with another woman.

We find reprehensible these and all the actions in the life of Fr. Maciel that were contrary to his Christian, religious, and priestly duties. We declare that they are not what we strive to live in the Legion of Christ and in the Regnum Christi Movement.

2. The Legion of Christ and the Regnum Christi Movement in the face of these facts

Once again, we express our sorrow and grief to each and every person damaged by our founder's actions.
We share in the suffering this scandal has caused the Church, and it grieves and hurts us deeply.

We ask all those who accused him in the past to forgive us, those whom we did not believe or were incapable of giving a hearing to, since at the time we could not imagine that such behavior took place. If it turns out that anyone culpably cooperated in his misdeeds we will act according to the principles of Christian justice and charity, holding these people responsible for their actions.

We also ask our families, friends and benefactors to forgive us, and all other people of good will who have felt that their trust has been wounded. In addition, as members of the Mystical Body of Christ we feel the need to expiate his sins and the scandal they caused, making reparation with a

Christian spirit. We ask all the members of our religious family to intensify their prayer and sacrifice.

It is also our Christian and priestly duty to continue reaching out to those who have been affected in any way. Our greatest concern is for them, and we continue to offer them whatever spiritual and pastoral help they need, hoping thus to contribute to the necessary Christian reconciliation. At the same time, we know that only Christ is able to bring definitive healing and "make all things new" (cf. Rev. 21:5).

For his own mysterious reasons, God chose Fr. Maciel as an instrument to found the Legion of Christ and Regnum Christi, and we thank God for the good he did. At the same time, we accept and regret that, given the gravity of his faults, we cannot take his person as a model of Christian or priestly life. Christ condemns the sin but seeks to save the sinner. We take him as our model, convinced of the meaning and beauty of forgiveness, and we entrust our founder to God's merciful love.

3. The apostolic visitation
We wish to express our gratitude to the Holy Father, Pope Benedict XVI, not only for renewing "his solidarity and prayers in these delicate moments" (cf. Letter of Cardinal Tarcisio Bertone, SDB, to Fr. Alvaro Corcuera, March 10, 2009), but also for offering us the Apostolic Visitation as a

means to help us "overcome the present difficulties" (ibid.). Thus we hope to take the necessary steps to reinforce our foundations, formation and daily life as Legionaries of Christ and Regnum Christi members.

We thank the five apostolic Visitators, Bishop Giuseppe Versaldi, Archbishop Ricardo Blázquez, Archbishop Charles Chaput, OFM Cap., Archbishop Ricardo Ezzati, SDB, and Bishop Ricardo Watty, MSSP, for all the work they have done with such dedication and fatherly concern.

We will embrace with filial obedience whatever indications and recommendations the Holy Father gives us as a result of the apostolic visitation, and we are committed to putting them into practice.

4. Looking toward the future

In the time since January 2005 when we held our last General Chapter and Fr. Alvaro Corcuera, LC, was elected as our general director, we have striven to guide the Legion of Christ and Regnum Christi in fidelity to all we have received from God and has been approved by the Church. Humbly and gratefully we acknowledge the blessings and fruits that the Lord has granted us up to now, and we accept our responsibility to deepen our understanding of our history, charism, and spirituality.

We face the future with hope, knowing that our one support is God. We trust totally in him and in his all-powerful love which, as St Paul says, "makes all things work for the good of those who love him" (Rom. 8:28). We know that as we follow this path we will be aided by the Holy Spirit and the Church's motherly guidance.

Our purpose as individuals and as an institution is to love Christ, live his Gospel, and extend throughout the world his Kingdom of peace and love. We know that if we are to do this we must constantly renew ourselves as individuals and as a community, in fidelity to the tradition of consecrated life, the better to serve the Church and society. The past months have helped us to reflect on our identity and mission, and they have also moved us to review various aspects of our institutional life, humbly and in all simplicity.

We are resolved, among other things, to:

- Continue seeking reconciliation and reaching out to those who have suffered,

- Honor the truth about our history,

- Continue offering safety, especially for minors, in our institutions and activities, both in environments and in procedures,

- Grow in a spirit of unselfish service to the Church and people,

- Cooperate better with all the bishops and with other institutions in the Church,

- Improve our communication,

- Continue our oversight to insure that our administrative controls and procedures are implemented on all levels, and to continue demanding proper accountability,

- Redouble our dedication to the mission of offering Christ's Gospel to as many people as possible,

- And above all, seek holiness with renewed effort, guided by the Church.

Conclusion

We cannot end this communiqué without thanking the thousands of Legionaries, consecrated men and women and all Regnum Christi members who have given and continue to give their lives to God in the service of the Church and society with absolute generosity, and all those who work in our centers and works of apostolate. Thanks to you and your work, we can say that today Christ is more known and loved in the world. We also express our gratitude toward every person that has always been there to support us with their faith, prayers and suffering united to Christ's.

Signed today, March 25, the solemnity of the Annunciation of Our Lord. Through the intercession of his Mother, the Blessed Virgin Mary, may the Lord grant us the grace to enter ever more deeply into the mystery of the Love of God made man, and to live and share it with renewed fervor.

Fr. Álvaro Corcuera, LC, general director
Fr. Luis Garza, LC, vicar general
Fr. Francisco Mateos, LC, general counselor
Fr. Michael Ryan, LC, general counselor
Fr. Joseph Burtka, LC, general counselor
Fr. Evaristo Sada, LC, general secretary
Fr. José Cárdenas, LC, territorial director for Chile and Argentina
Fr. José Manuel Otaolaurruchi, LC, territorial director for Venezuela and Colombia
Fr. Manuel Aromir, LC, territorial director for Brazil
Fr. Rodolfo Mayagoitia, LC, territorial director for Mexico and Central America
Fr. Leonardo Nuñez, LC, territorial director for Monterrey
Fr. Scott Reilly, LC, territorial director for Atlanta
Fr. Julio Martí, LC, territorial director for New York
Fr. Jesús María Delgado, LC, territorial director for Spain
Fr. Jacobo Muñoz, LC, territorial director for France and Ireland
Fr. Sylvester Heereman, territorial director for Germany and Central Europe

8

Official Text of the Findings of the 2009-2010 Vatican "Visitation" of the Legion of Christ

Rereading something I have read so many times I am struck by how the last part of my correspondence with Fr. Neuhaus may be an excellent segue to this investigation into the Legion of Christ. The « Visitation », announced in March, 2009, officially launched on July 15 of the same year, concluded its first stage with the delivery of documents to the Vatican on March 15, 2010.

Fr. Neuhaus had asked almost rhetorically: What did they (the victim accusers) expect from the Vatican? The question initially stunned me by its bluntness and I scrambled to formulate a reply that would do justice to the various layers of people who believe they have been unjustly treated or abused by Fr. Maciel and his Work.

The victim accusers wanted Fr. Maciel to be severely punished by Church authorities before he died. Fr. Maciel passed on without acknowledging his sins and without apologizing to his victims.

They wanted the Vatican to review the Constitutions and Traditions of the Legion, and to investigate and reform Legion recruitment, training, retaining and dismissal practices; to have a "clean" General Chapter without the ever- present pressure and control of Maciel. After the death of the founder this would mean for them the exclusion of Maciel's direct appointees, i.e. the present leadership cadre.

Many former Legion and Regnum Christi members wanted church authorities to examine and investigate Fr. Maciel's creation, the Legionaries of Christ and its Regnum Christi Movement, particularly the way it recruits, retains, controls members, and also how it handles dissident and exiting members. There were serious concerns about the way Fr. Maciel and the Legion fundraised and used monies. Could the 2009-2010 Vatican Visitation of the Legion of Christ be a response to these requests, an answer to these prayers?

COMMUNIQUE OF VISITATORS OF LEGIONARIES OF CHRIST

VATICAN CITY, 1 MAY 2010 (VIS) –

The Holy See Press Office today published the following communiqué:

1. On 30 April and 1 May, the cardinal secretary of State chaired a meeting at the Vatican with the five bishops in charge of the apostolic visitation of the Congregation of the Legionaries of Christ (Archbishop Ricardo Blazquez Perez of Valladolid, Spain; Archbishop Charles Joseph Chaput O.F.M. Cap. of Denver; Archbishop Ricardo Ezzati Andrello S.D.B., of Concepcion, Chile; Bishop Giuseppe Versaldi of Alexandria, Italy; and Bishop Ricardo Watty Urquidi M.Sp.S, of Tepic, Mexico). The meeting was also attended by the prefect of the Congregation for the Doctrine of the Faith, the prefect of the Congregation for Institutes of Consecrated Life and Societies of Apostolic Life, and the substitute of the Section for General Affairs of the Secretariat of State.

The Holy Father was present at one of the sessions, at which the visitors presented a summary of their reports, which had already been previously delivered.

During the visitation more than 1,000 Legionaries were interviewed, and hundreds of written testimonies examined. The visitors went to almost all the religious houses and many of the apostolic works run by the congregation. They heard, orally or in writing, the opinion of many diocesan bishops of the countries in which the congregation works. The visitors also met many members of the "Regnum Christi" Movement - although it was not the subject of the visitation - especially consecrated men and women. They have also received a great amount of correspondence from lay people and family members of those involved in the movement.

The five Visitators spoke of the warm welcome they received and of the constructive spirit of co-operation shown by the congregation and the individual religious. Though each Visitator acted independently, they came to substantial agreement and a shared viewpoint in their assessments. They testified to having met a great number of exemplary religious who are honest and talented, many of them young, who seek Christ with genuine zeal and are offering their entire lives to spread the Kingdom of God.

2. The apostolic visit was able to ascertain that the behaviour of Fr. Marcial Maciel Degollado has had serious consequences for the life and structure of the Legion, such as to require a process of in-depth revision.

The very serious and objectively immoral behaviour of Fr. Maciel, as incontrovertible evidence has confirmed, sometimes resulted in actual crimes, and manifests a life devoid of scruple and of genuine religious sentiment. The great majority of Legionaries were unaware of this life, above all because of the system of relationships created by Fr. Maciel, who had skillfully managed to build up alibis, to gain the trust, confidence and silence of those around him, and to strengthen his role as a charismatic founder.

Not infrequently, the lamentable discrediting and dismissal of whoever doubted the correctness of his behaviour, coupled with the misguided conviction of not wanting to harm the good the Legion was doing, created a defense mechanism around Fr. Maciel that rendered him untouchable for a long time and made it very difficult to know his real life.

3. The sincere zeal of most Legionaries, which emerged in the visits to the houses of the congregation and to many of its widely-appreciated apostolic works, has in the past led many people to believe that the allegations, which gradually became more insistent and widespread, could not have been anything other than calumnies.

Thus, discovering and coming to know the truth about the founder has caused the members of the Legion surprise, bewilderment and deep pain, as the Visitators have made clear.

4. From the results of the apostolic visitation the following elements, among others, have become clear:

a) The need to redefine the charism of the Congregation of the Legionaries of Christ, preserving its true core, that of the "militia Christi", which characterises the apostolic and missionary activity of the Church and which is not the same as efficiency at any cost.

b) The need to review the exercise of authority, which must be linked to truth, in order to respect conscience and develop in the light of the Gospel as authentic ecclesial service.

c) The need to preserve, through appropriate formation, the enthusiasm of the faith of young members, their missionary zeal and their apostolic dynamism. Disillusionment concerning the founder could call into question this vocation and the core of the charism which belongs to and distinguishes the Legionaries of Christ.

5. The Holy Father wishes to assure all Legionaries and members of the "Regnum Christi" Movement that they will not be abandoned. The Church is firmly resolved to accompany them and help them on the path of purification that awaits them. This will also mean dealing sincerely with all of those who, within and outside the Legion, were victims of sexual abuse and of the power system devised by the founder. They are in the Holy Father's thoughts and prayers at this time, along with his gratitude to those of them who, even in the midst of great difficulties, had the courage and constancy to demand the truth.

6. The Holy Father, in thanking the Visitators for the sensitive task they have accomplished with skill, generosity, and profound pastoral sensitivity,

reserves to himself the task of soon instructing how this assistance will be organised, beginning with the appointment of a delegate of his own and a commission to study the Legion's constitutions.

The Holy Father will send a Visitator to the consecrated members of the "Regnum Christi" Movement, who have insistently requested this.

7. Finally, the Pope renews his encouragement to all the Legionaries of Christ, to their families, and to all the lay people involved in the "Regnum Christi" Movement, during this difficult time for the congregation and for each of them. He urges them not to lose sight of the fact that their vocation, which originates in Christ's call and is driven by the ideal of being witnesses of His love to the world, is a genuine gift from God, a treasure for the Church, and the indestructible foundation upon which each of them can build their own future and that of the Legion.

OP/ VIS 20100503 (1040)
Published by VIS - Holy See Press Office - Monday, May 03, 2010

9

And Pope Benedict XVI said in *Light of the World*[19] ...

Who would have ever dreamt that the pope would directly address the Marcial Maciel issue in the context of priestly sexual abuse and the Church crisis? But thanks to a resourceful reporter and an intrepid pope this has become a reality. The reader has already seen snippets and heard sound bites in the media. Let the pope's full words stand by themselves in their clarity and force.

In *Light of the World*, the Maciel scandal is not addressed in Chapter 2, *The Abuse Scandal*, where one might expect to find it but rather in Chapter 3, *Causes of the Crisis and New Opportunity*. However, in Chapter 2 Benedict prepares the way: "You are right: it is a particularly serious sin when someone who is actually supposed to help people toward God, to whom a child or a young person is entrusted in order to find the Lord, abuses him instead and leads him away from the Lord. As a result the faith as such becomes unbelievable, and the Church can no longer present itself credibly as the herald of the Lord. All this shocked us and very deeply upsets me now as before. However, the

---

[19] *The Pope, the Church, and the Signs of the Times, A Conversation with Peter Seewald*, 2010, Ignatius Press, San Francisco.

Lord told us that among the wheat there will be weeds –but that the seed, his seed, will nevertheless continue to grow. We are confident of that."

The pope is asked: *And nevertheless it is difficult for many people these days to stand by the Church. Can you understand why people respond by leaving in protest?*

"I can understand it. I am thinking of course above all about the victims themselves. That it is difficult for them to keep believing that the Church is a source of good, that she communicates the light of Christ, that she helps people in life –I can understand that. And others, who have only these negative perceptions, no longer see the overall picture, the life of the Church. All the more reason that the Church must strive to make this vitality and greatness visible again, despite all that is negative."

Chapter 3 is introduced by the interviewer:
You pronounced an unforgettable indictment during the Stations of the Cross on Good Friday of 2005, a few weeks before you were elected the successor of John Paul II: "How often do we celebrate only ourselves without even realizing that he is there! How often is his Word twisted and misused! How much filth there is in the Church, and even among those who, in the priesthood, ought to belong entirely to him!"

"(...) That is a question that really touches on the *mysterium iniquitatis*, the mystery of evil. One wonders also in this regard: What does someone like that think in the morning when he goes to the altar and offers the Holy Sacrifice? Does he actually go to confession? What does he say in confession? What consequences does that confession have for him? It really ought to be a major factor in extricating him from it and compelling him to amend his life. It is a mystery that someone who has pledged himself to what is holy can lose it so completely and then, indeed, can lose his origins. At his priestly ordination he must have had at least a longing for what is great and pure; otherwise he would not have made that choice. How can someone fall so far?"

Author replies to Pope

I must respond to the above words of his Holiness. The good pope is speaking from a perspective of faith, decency, and normalcy. From thence he cannot comprehend a scoundrel like Marcial Maciel. Fr. Marcial Maciel did not go every morning to the altar to offer the Holy Sacrifice of the Mass. All of us who lived under the same roof with him know this to be a fact. In the first place Nuestro Padre spent most of his time traveling to various countries or resting at unknown destinations -some of the superiors had to know his whereabouts. As a simple member of the community I had no idea where he was for the most part. The remainder of his time, when he was living in one of the main centers –in his own special quarters- was spent either in his room where he was "sick" or "taking care of important business". He would go days, weeks without saying mass. He might say mass for a special occasion or feast day. He always needed someone -master of ceremonies- to closely guide through the mass ritual and prayers, as if he were not familiar with them. He never went to confession that I know of. This simple reality dispatches the pope's other pious considerations re the sacrament of penance. What was Fr. Maciel thinking during his priestly ordination? Only God knows. His priestly ordination was a step in the direction of being the founder of his new order. We know that his philosophical and theological studies were piecemeal and his bishop uncle, Monsignor Arias, was the one who put him through and ordained him. Perhaps another bishop might not have been so accommodating. But Marcial was a genius at getting what he wanted. The pope continues:

"(…) Evil, too, will always be part of the mystery of the Church. And when we see what men, what the clergy have done in the Church, then that is nothing short of proof that he founded and upholds the Church. If she were dependent on men, she would long since have perished."

Regarding Fr. Marcial Maciel

The interviewer:
The Church was shaken also by revelations about the double life of Marcial Maciel Degollado, the founder of a religious congregation of priests, the Legion of Christ. Sexual abuse accusations against Maciel, who died in 2008 in the United States, had already been in place for years. Maciel's partner

stated that she is the mother of two of his children. Some voices in Mexico now are claiming that the public apologies of the Legionaries of Christ are not sufficient, that the congregation must be dissolved. His Holiness:

"Unfortunately we addressed these things very slowly and late. Somehow they were concealed very well, and only around the year 2000 did we have concrete clues. Ultimately unequivocal evidence was needed in order to be sure that the accusations were grounded. To me Marcial Maciel remains a mysterious figure. There is, on the one hand, a life that, as we now know, was out of moral bounds – an adventurous, wasted twisted life. On the other hand, we see the dynamism and the strength with which he built up the congregation of Legionaries. (...)"

Author Questions Pope

It is a relief to know that in these considerations the Pope is not infallible and can be questioned. What is incredible is the seeming sensibleness and silkiness of his words. There is a slight admission of neglect or inefficiency. What can be read between the lines is that the Vatican and the pope tried as hard as they could to defend and protect Fr. Maciel against the amounting heap of evidence, to minimize the nature of his "sins", and to save the "Work of God" that he had created. The pope takes refuge in a quasi-biblical image of "a mysterious figure." But such a figure is in total contrast to the Christ-like biblical figure of "The Son of Man" of the Synoptic Gospels and the "Suffering Servant" of the Second-Isaiah. Mention of such brings to mind Fr. Maciel's –and the Legion's- blasphemous attributions of Christ-like suffering attributed to the founder soon after he was censored by the Vatican in 2006:

Fr. Maciel, with the spirit of obedience to the Church that has always characterized him, has accepted this communiqué with faith, complete serenity, and tranquility of conscience, knowing that it is a new cross that God, the Father of Mercy, has allowed him to suffer and that will obtain many graces for the Legion of Christ and the Regnum Christi Movement.[20]

The pope defines Fr. Maciel's existence as "a life that was out of moral bounds- an adventurous, wasted twisted life." He treads too lightly. Because Fr. Maciel was much worse than that; he was a veritably depraved hypocrite, whose reality far outshone Molière's fictional Tartuffe. He was guilty of sexually abusing his own seminarians, of using them in diverse ways, of masquerading as a saint and a holy priest, of lying and deceiving, of being a totally self-centered and narcissistic person, of being cruel and vengeful, of punishing and exiling those who did not agree with him or wanted to hold him accountable, of manipulating popes and cardinals, of infiltrating the departments of the Roman Curia to gather information for his schemes

---

[20] http://www.zenit.org/article-16068?l=english

and to cover his traces. He entered into fraudulent sexual relationships with at least two women and had children by them. It has even been reported that he sexually abused his own male children.

His Holiness grasps at the paradox, that "quel paradoxe!" so beloved by the French. "On the other hand, we see the dynamism and the strength with which he build up the congregation of the Legionaries".

It is a very hard sell. How could this moral monster found a religious order? Are you asking us to believe that the Holy Spirit founded the Legion of Christ despite the moral corruption of the founder? Or that Maciel was satyr and saint at the same time, in an allusion to the nature of the Church herself as the whore-virgin, *Casta Meretrix* postulated by Hans Urs von Balthasar?

Now you have given me pause....

10

Paradox envisioned by Benedict, unseen by Neuhaus

Richard John Neuhaus wrote

"Common sense is also entered into evidence. Is it believable that, as alleged, a pathological, drug–addicted child molester could have founded a religious order in the 1940s that was approved by the Church and flourished for decades, while all the time casual sodomy and other heinous sexual abuses reigned in its houses? And this without a word of concern from thousands of parents or any claim of such wrongdoing in civil, criminal, or ecclesiastical courts? It is not believable. Is it believable that men who are now accusers, who were then adult members of the order, would have testified under oath to Fr. Maciel's uprightness, thus lying to their highest superiors in the Holy See and refusing to mention years of abuse by a drug–addicted molester who had been removed as head of the order? It is not believable. The accusations are odious, as are the actions of those who continue to peddle them.

The accusers may say that they are seeking justice or, in the psychobabble of our time, looking for "closure." I cannot plumb their motives. I do not know what grievances, grudges, or vendettas are in play here, or what memories or "recovered memories" are reflected in the accusations. The accusers are not going to court to seek damages of any sort. That is not a possibility. The sole end served by the charges is the attempt to gravely damage the Legionaries of Christ by discrediting their founder.

I am confident they will not succeed in that attempt. Because the accusations are false, and will be recognized as such by any fair–minded person who bothers to look into them. And because the Legionaries are so manifestly, capably, and joyfully determined to pursue their apostolate, undistracted by the opposition that is predictably encountered by any young and vigorous movement of renewal. To be sure, there are still those feathers of scandal scattered about. St. Philip Neri was right, it is probably impossible to collect all of them. But if you come across one, just pick it up and put it in the trash where it belongs."

Benedict XVI says

"Meanwhile we have had an Apostolic Visitation carried out and appointed a delegate who together with a group of collaborators is preparing the necessary reforms. Naturally, corrections must be made, but by and large, the congregation is sound. In it there are many young men who enthusiastically want to serve the faith. This enthusiasm must not be destroyed. Many of them have been called by a false figure to what is, in the end, right after all.

That is the remarkable thing, the paradox, that a false prophet, so to speak, could still have a positive effect."

Your Holiness

That is the question. Can a false prophet do the work of God? You answer in the affirmative. Your biblical, patristic, and church history studies allow you to make that affirmation. Can a corrupt priest found a bona fide religious order? We know he can make the Eucharist and forgive sins. But what if he abuses the sacrament of confession with "sollicitatio complicis"? What if he solicits altar boys before going out onto the altar? What about these abominations which cry to God for redress?

Holy Father, forgive my lack of faith!

And what if we look outside your box, the box of scholastic philosophy and theology, of patristic studies, of church history or moral theology and move into the realm of psychology, sociology, and criminology? We go beyond the concept of sinner, twisted life, bad priest, unscrupulous religious and move into the realm of pedophile, psychopath, and anti-social personality disorder.

A final word; it seems that nobody at the Vatican wants to contemplate another possibility: what if Fr. Maciel, the pedophile psychopath conman was also a guru who founded a control-obsessed secretive sect? What if a cult could spring up not only outside the Catholic Church but within in own bosom? ReGAIN, the nonprofit legally assailed by the Legion in 2007 for "maliciously slandering Fr. Maciel and publishing the Legion's proprietary materials" has been planting the seeds of that doubt for years.

Occasionally, a courageous Catholic bishop will point to the elephant in the kitchen:

In an interview, then Archbishop of Baltimore, Edwin F. O'Brien acknowledged that "while there are faithful priests in the Legion, he is concerned that the movement fosters a 'cult of personality' with Fr. Maciel, in the center."

"While it's difficult to get a hold of official documents," Archbishop O'Brien noted, "it's clear that from the first moment a person joins the Legion, efforts seem to be made to program each one and to gain full control of his behavior, of all information he receives, of his thinking and emotions."

He continued by noting that when members of the Legion have left, many have suffered "deep psychological distress for dependency and need prolonged counseling akin to deprogramming."[21]

---

[21]http://www.catholicreview.org/subpages/storyworldnew -new.aspx?action=5703

And, Your Holiness, you are indirectly giving your interpretation to the words of Our Savior, Matthew, chapter 7, Sermon on the Mount:

17 Likewise every good tree bears good fruit, but a bad tree bears bad fruit. 18 A good tree cannot bear bad fruit, and a bad tree cannot bear good fruit. 19 Every tree that does not bear good fruit is cut down and thrown into the fire. 20 Thus, by their fruit you will recognize them.

According to Your Holiness, the bad tree can bear good fruit. And therein stands or falls your diagnosis and treatment of the Legion of Christ.

The doubting, questioning, once-bitten-twice-shy survivor part of me rears its ugly head again just as it did way back in my Legion days prompting me to object:

Or did the madman create something mad? Did the depraved man create something depraved? Did the Great Deceiver create something deceiving? Did the Great Exploiter create an exploiting organization? Did the Abuser create an organization that continues to seduce, abuse, and corrupt its own members, their relatives and the unsuspecting Catholic faithful? Does the Illusionist continue to dazzle the Catholic hierarchy, including you, Pope Benedict XVI?

11

Diagnosing Maciel

There are not many sources for the English-speaking public to gather an idea of Marcial Maciel in his daily life as a person, priest, superior, and founder. The myth has prevailed. However, some firsthand testimonies have appeared over the years. Two of his sexual victims have produced memoirs in Spanish: Alejandro Espinosa (2003) with *El Legionario* and Francisco González Parga (2010) with *Yo Acuso al Padre Maciel y a la Legión de Cristo* describing in detail his sexual abuse of them and others from that generation. These testimonies can be emotionally revulsive and are not for the faint of heart.

Quite a number of historical, psychological and sociological studies have seen the light in Spanish, most of which I mention at the end of my memoir and study of our leading man, *Our Father Maciel who art in bed, a Naïve and Sentimental Dubliner in the Legion of Christ* (2008, book and Kindle). There I described some of Fr. Maciel's selfish, petty, nasty, and cruel features, long before it was permitted to criticize such an untouchable figure in the American Catholic world. Berry Renner's 2004 *Vows of Silence* was the first English language book that studied Maciel and the Legion in some depth, putting the pedophilia accusations center stage. Berry (2011) recently published *Render unto Rome* where he devotes a chapter to Maciel's devious role in Legion administration and finances. An Irish-born former Legionary from my generation, Jack Keogh, who knew and collaborated with Fr. Maciel, published *Driving Straight on Crooked Lines: How an Irishman found his heart and nearly lost his mind* (2010). Despite wanting to maintain a cool and objective stance Keogh has to acknowledge some of Maciel's twistedness.

In these books, in articles, and essays attempts have been made to name Maciel's shamelessness. One can take a religious, moral, legal, sociological or psychological approach. As psychotherapy is my métier I have taken the latter tack. For decades I have listened to victims face to face and read testimonies in English and especially in Spanish in an effort to understand the Maciel phenomenon. In my correspondence with Fr. Richard John Neuhaus I focused on Maciel as a sexual abuser, a peculiar brand of pedophile. Recent statements by the Legion acknowledged that Fr. Maciel took advantage of younger gullible women in emotional and sexual ways. It seems he also sexually abused his own flesh and blood. One of his son's is suing the Legion.

From the beginning I held that Fr. Maciel's "illness" was more than some sick sexual perversion; it was broader and deeper in scope. Juan Jose Vaca, one of his victims, believes Maciel suffered from Malignant Narcissism[22]. In fact, Pedophilia and Narcissism have in common the gratification of the self to the

---

[22]Malignant narcissism has been described as "an extreme form of antisocial personality disorder that is manifest in a person who is pathologically grandiose, lacking in conscience and behavioral regulation, and with characteristic demonstrations of joyful cruelty and sadism". http://en.wikipedia.org/wiki/Malignant_narcissism

detriment of others. Peter Kingsland, father of a Regnum Christi consecrated female, finds that the pervasive Narcissism described by Richard Boyd in *Narcissism as Prophesy* fits Maciel to a tee: *But know this, that in the last days grievous times shall come. For men shall be lovers of self, lovers of money, boastful, haughty, blasphemers, disobedient to parents, unthankful, unholy, without natural affections, implacable, slanderers, without control, fierce, no lovers of good, traitors, headstrong, puffed up, lovers of pleasure rather than lovers of God; holding a form of godliness, but having denied the power thereof.* (2 Tim 3, 1-5)

Maciel's basic characteristic was has his almost diabolical knack for lying and deceiving, his unbridled ambition and lust for power, and his total disregard for others' feelings, rights and well-being. I believe the mental health diagnosis that best describes Marcial Maciel's modus operandi is Antisocial Personality Disorder. The term has a drawback in that people may focus on the word "antisocial" and mistake it for "asocial", socially withdrawn, which Maciel was certainly not; indeed, he needed people to exploit them. Antisocial personality disorder (ASPD) is described by the American Psychiatric Association's Diagnostic and Statistical Manual, fourth edition (DSM-IV-TR), as an Axis II personality disorder characterized by "...a pervasive pattern of disregard for, and violation of, the rights of others that begins in childhood or early adolescence and continues into adulthood..."[23]

Psychopathy and sociopathy are terms related to

---

[23] See Addendum 5, page 117, Antisocial Personality Disorder

ASPD. ASPD replaced psychopathy as a diagnosis in the DSM but the terms are not identical. Psychopathy is now (like sociopathy) usually seen as a subset of ASPD. Many people with ASPD are not violent unless significantly and specifically provoked. I have not used ASD in the title for clarity sake and as a way of drawing the attention to the fact that Maciel was not simply a sexual deviant.

Perhaps Marcial Maciel's "illness" was not unique; other sociopaths have disgraced the world's and the Church's stage over the course of history. What contributed to his uniqueness are at least two other factors: that this psychopath possessed extraordinary ambition, need for control and power, and marvelous entrepreneurial skills; and that despite being a pan-sexual predator he was able to be ordained to the Catholic priesthood and allowed to found a religious order. From this prestigious position he could indulge his vices and apply a business model to the recruitment, training, fundraising and works of the Legion of Christ and Regnum Christi Movement. Very few people tried to expose Maciel during his life. The Vatican for the most part defended Maciel, protected him, and eventually, when confronted with the evidence of its own investigation, let him off lightly. The Legion closed ranks in blind obedience. A few "cult watchdogs"[24] smelled a rat but few inside the Church paid much attention to them −except the unfortunate parents who had given their children to

---

[24]Steven Hassan, http://www.freedomofmind.com/ Rick Ross, http://www.rickross.com/ sites have long been on the Legion's trail and can be very useful to members, relatives, and helping professionals.

the Legion and the Regnum and wanted to recover them! A few railing prophets like Barba, Lennon, and Vaca cried out in the wilderness but were branded and discarded as "disgruntled old men".

I do give credit to Pope Benedict XVI for breaking the taboo around Maciel and the Legion. In 2005 a Vatican investigator began prizing open the secret doors surrounding Maciel and found that skeletons really did exist in that closet. As his health deteriorated and his grip on men, women and institution weakened the containing walls The Founder built around him began to collapse. There came a point when his past caught up with him and he was no longer able to keep the filth from oozing out. And when, for some as yet unknown reason, Legion leadership decided to reveal Maciel's dalliances with women and acknowledged other crimes "all hell broke loose" in the media and in Rome. The heretofore inexpugnable Legion was breached in 2009 when the Vatican launched an investigation into the organization and "visitors" discovered discontented souls gliding silently along the corridors of the isolated compound.

APPENDIX

Addendum I,

September 17, 2004

(Author's journal entry)

Pedophilia Epidemic

Since originally drafting this letter to the editor some months ago (September 2004), I have learned that another serious epidemic of pedophilia struck the Apostolic School in Ontaneda, Santander, Spain in recent years, causing the institution to be closed down. This is one of the reasons I and others are concerned that Father Maciel, because of his influence in the Vatican, is getting off Scot free and that, subsequently, sexual abuse is being condoned from generation to generation in the Legion. You do understand now how important it is for Father Maciel to totally deny the allegations and discredit his accusers! Otherwise, well-meaning people like you will, sooner or later, start to question...

Addendum 2

September, 2004

(Author's journal entry)

An Enigma to Me

I had felt Nuestro Padre's verbal and emotional abuse of myself and other confreres over the years. More than that, I had experienced his leadership style which I knew could be ruthless and full of disregard for feelings and dignity, a kind of coldness and cruelty, which shocked me in a person considered a saint. I knew he would stop at nothing to reach his goals. Thus, I gradually lost my esteem for Father Maciel over the course of my 23 years in the Legion. Nothing would surprise me about him. But I had no conscious experience or awareness of his sexual wrongdoing. The accusations of sexual abuse, for me, however, were not so much a purely sexual thing, nor a questioning of his holiness - I was sure he had none - but rather: was Father Maciel capable of misusing his power to this extent? Although I had never thought of Our Father as a sexual predator, I always had questions about his psycho-sexual make up, his - to me - "strangeness". He always seemed to be cut off or disconnected from his deep or tender feelings, from what I would consider "normal" emotions. I had often heard him express himself with contempt about women. Because of my own very affectionate nature, I could never understand his affectivity: whether he had one in the ordinary sense of the word: whether he really "cared" about anyone. It seemed like he "used" people. And I had always been struck by Augustine's: "Use things, love people." I had never met a person quite like Maciel before, and often wondered "what made him tick". Or was he always "on guard" around others, always calculating, scheming? Could he be so controlling of his own emotions, in all his human relationships and interactions?

Addendum 3

October 18, 2004

(Author's journal entry)

Maciel's Favoritism

I remember very clearly that Raul de Anda, LC, a dark and handsome Mexican with fine features, was his personal secretary for a period in the 60s in Rome. Juan Manuel Correa, another Mexican, was a butler to Nuestro Padre. We three were students together at Via Aurelia 677. Padre Raul, - in the LC Theology students are called "Padre" - is now Dr. Raul de Anda, thanks to a PhD in experimental psychology. He was never ordained, and after leaving the Legion remained on good terms with Fr. Maciel. He is one of the "psychologists" to whom Legion superiors will refer suffering members. Raul, then --as now-- a Legion employee, worked at the LC Marriage and Family Center in Mexico City, "ALFA Y OMEGA" in the mid to late 70's just as the School of Faith -my apostolate- was taking shape a few blocks away in the wealthy Lomas de Chapultepec neighborhood. Fr. Juan Manuel Fernandez-Amenábar, later a Maciel accuser, - because of his personal charm with Mexican upper class women, their husbands and purse strings - was appointed founder, chaplain, spiritual director and lecturer at ALFA Y OMEGA by Fr. Maciel.

The "favoritism" I referred to above happened within my own group of candidates, novices and humanities students (1961-63). Fr. Maciel did single out one or two in our group of eight co-founders and give them preferential treatment: more individual attention, confidences, greater access to his private quarters, special assignments, more travel, time with their family and the "privilege" of traveling with him as his personal secretary. During these times of "accompanying Nuestro Padre", the religious were totally unsupervised and "dispensed" from the normal duties of the religious life, sometimes even neglecting their "Acts of Piety", prayer life. These seminarians are now in their 60s. Some are still in the Legion and others have left. None of them have wanted to comment on the sexual abuse issue, except the odd one who allowed his name to be used in the official LC "conspiracy theory" which pretended to discredit the accusers.

Addendum 4

January 27, 2005

(Author's journal entry)

When I met Felix Alarcón in Pontevedra, Spain, in May 2003, he spoke about Juan José Vaca's accusations in the diocese of Rockville Center. The bishop, who had known Felix before Vaca and held him in high regard contacted him and questioned him about Vaca and these incredible accusations. Alarcón, who had never addressed that issue before, had to admit that the accusations were true. From then on, Fr. Alarcón began to accept his victimhood and responsibility in the abuse at Via Aurelia 677. "If it were not for Juan José Vaca –he revealed emotionally- I would have carried that secret to my grave!"

Addendum 5

Antisocial Personality Disorder[25]

DSM-IV

The Diagnostic and Statistical Manual of Mental Disorders, fourth edition (DSM IV-TR), defines antisocial personality disorder (in Axis II Cluster B) as:

A) There is a pervasive pattern of disregard for and violation of the rights of others occurring since age 15 years, as indicated by three or more of the following:

failure to conform to social norms with respect to lawful behaviors as indicated by repeatedly performing acts that are grounds for arrest;

deception, as indicated by repeatedly lying, use of aliases, or conning others for personal profit or pleasure;

impulsiveness or failure to plan ahead;

irritability and aggressiveness, as indicated by repeated physical fights or assaults;

reckless disregard for safety of self or others;

consistent irresponsibility, as indicated by repeated failure to sustain consistent work behavior or honor financial obligations;

lack of remorse, as indicated by being indifferent to or rationalizing having hurt, mistreated, or stolen from another;

B) The individual is at least age 18 years.

---

[25]http://en.wikipedia.org/wiki/Antisocial_personality_disorder

C) There is evidence of conduct disorder with onset before age 15 years.

D) The occurrence of antisocial behavior is not exclusively during the course of schizophrenia or a manic episode.

New evidence points to the possibility that children often develop antisocial personality disorder as a result of environmental as well as genetic influence. The individual must be at least 18 years of age to be diagnosed with this disorder (Criterion B), but those commonly diagnosed with ASPD as adults were diagnosed with conduct disorder as children. The prevalence of this disorder is 3% in males and 1% from females, as stated in the DSM IV-TR.

ICD-10

The World Health Organization's International Statistical Classification of Diseases and Related Health Problems, tenth edition (ICD-10), defines a conceptually similar disorder to antisocial personality disorder called (F60.2) Dissocial personality disorder.

It is characterized by at least 3 of the following:

Callous unconcern for the feelings of others and lack of the capacity for empathy.

Gross and persistent attitude of irresponsibility and disregard for social norms, rules, and obligations.

Incapacity to maintain enduring relationships.

Very low tolerance to frustration and a low threshold for discharge of aggression, including violence.

Incapacity to experience guilt and to profit from experience, particularly punishment.

Markedly prone to blame others or to offer plausible rationalizations for the behavior bringing the subject into conflict.

Persistent irritability.

The criteria specifically rule out conduct disorders. Dissocial personality disorder criteria differ from those for antisocial and sociopathic personality disorders.

It is a requirement of ICD-10 that a diagnosis of any specific personality disorder also satisfies a set of general personality disorder criteria.

CPSIA information can be obtained
at www.ICGtesting.com
Printed in the USA
LVHW091436111021
700143LV00015B/914

9 781475 215793